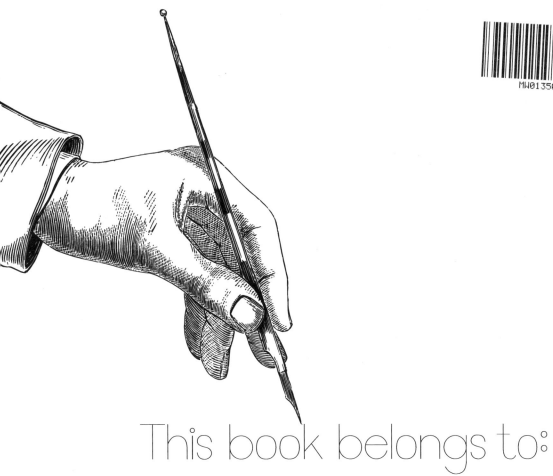

This book belongs to:

_____

Copyright© 2023 Seaside Study

All rights reserved. No part of this book may be reproduced, photocopied, or used in any manner without the prior written permission of the copyright owner, except for brief quotations in a book review.

Learn Handwriting
WITH
DRAWING

SEASIDE STUDY

TABLE OF CONTENTS

1 Chapter 1: Introduction and Warmup

In the opening chapter, we will equip you with essential handwriting tips, setting the stage for your journey towards success. Additionally, we'll offer you specialized handwriting warm-up pages to refine your hand control and prepare you for the writing and drawing adventure ahead.

9 Chapter 2: Letters

In this chapter, we'll be your guides as we explore the art of writing each letter with style and simplicity.

39 Chapter 3: Drawing and Writing

In Chapter Three, we're diving into fun activities! We'll practice our handwriting while drawing different animals. You'll also get to learn three great facts about each animal and improve your handwriting skills.

97 Chapter 4: Free Writing

Chapter four is all about creativity! It's your turn to have fun with free writing. You can use this space to draw and write your very own stories, or simply practice your skills in writing and drawing.

Chapter 1

Introduction and Warmup

Welcome to the world of handwriting mastery! In this first chapter, we're about to embark on a journey to help you become a handwriting expert. We'll start by sharing tips and advice on everything from how to hold your pencil just right to fun ways to improve your writing. But that's not all – at the end of this chapter, you'll find special handwriting warm-up pages to kickstart your practice. So, grab your favorite pen or pencil, and let's dive into the wonderful world of penmanship. Are you ready to make your handwriting shine? Let's get started!

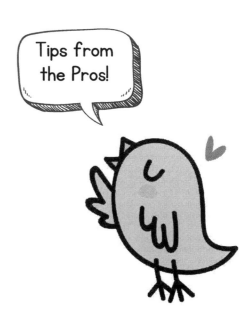

Tips from the Pros!

10 tips to improve handwriting

1. Posture Matters

Sit up straight with both feet flat on the ground. Good posture supports proper alignment of your hand and wrist, making it easier to control your movements.

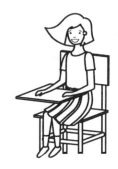

2. Relax Your Grip

Hold your pen or pencil gently, with your fingers forming a tripod grip (thumb and two fingers). Avoid gripping too tightly, which can lead to fatigue and cramped fingers.

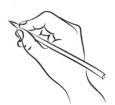

3. Consistency is Key

Strive for consistent letter size and spacing. This uniformity makes your handwriting more legible and aesthetically pleasing.

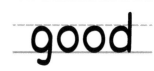

4. Sloped Writing

Angle your paper slightly to the left if you're right-handed and to the right if you're left-handed. This allows your hand to move more freely and reduces smudging.

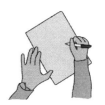

5. Practice Letter Formation

Pay attention to how each letter is formed. Consistent and correct letter formation is vital for legibility. Utilize lined paper to help with letter height and spacing.

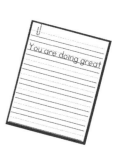

Handwriting tips and advice

6. Slow Down

Take your time when writing. Rushing can lead to sloppy handwriting. As you practice, you'll naturally become faster without sacrificing quality.

7. Use the Right Tools

Choose a pen or pencil that feels comfortable in your hand. Experiment with different writing instruments until you find the one that suits you best.

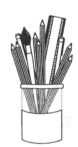

8. Warm-Up Exercises

Before you begin writing, do a few warm-up exercises to loosen your hand and wrist. Simple doodles and loops on your paper can help prepare your muscles for writing.

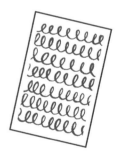

9. Patience and Perseverance

Remember that improving your handwriting takes time. Be patient with yourself and don't get discouraged by initial challenges.

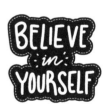

10. Seek Feedback

Ask friends, family, or teachers to review your handwriting and offer constructive feedback. Sometimes an outside perspective can help identify areas for improvement.

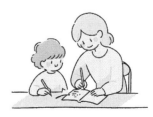

Trace the lines and patterns

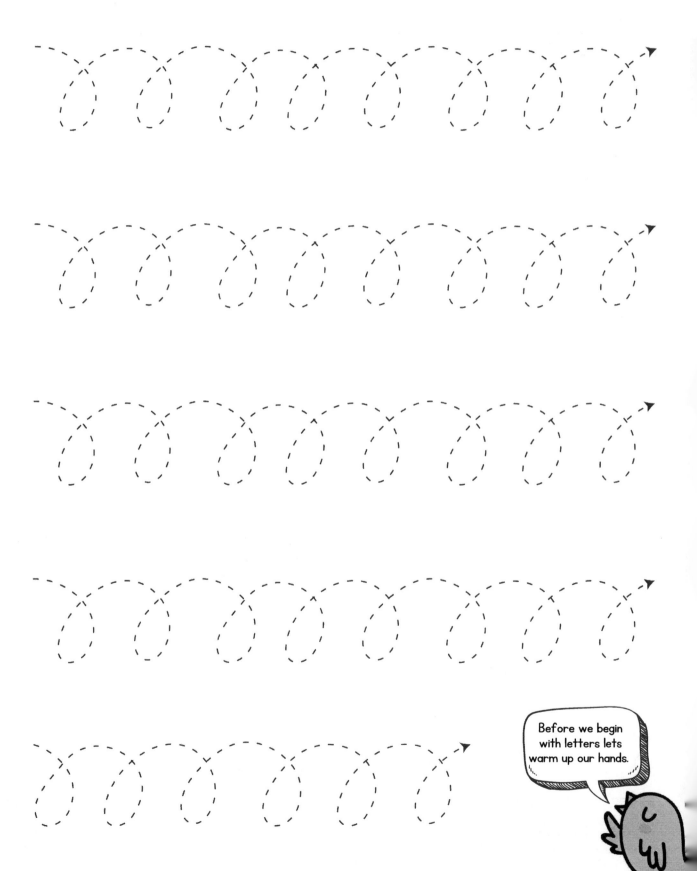

Before we begin with letters lets warm up our hands.

Trace the lines and patterns

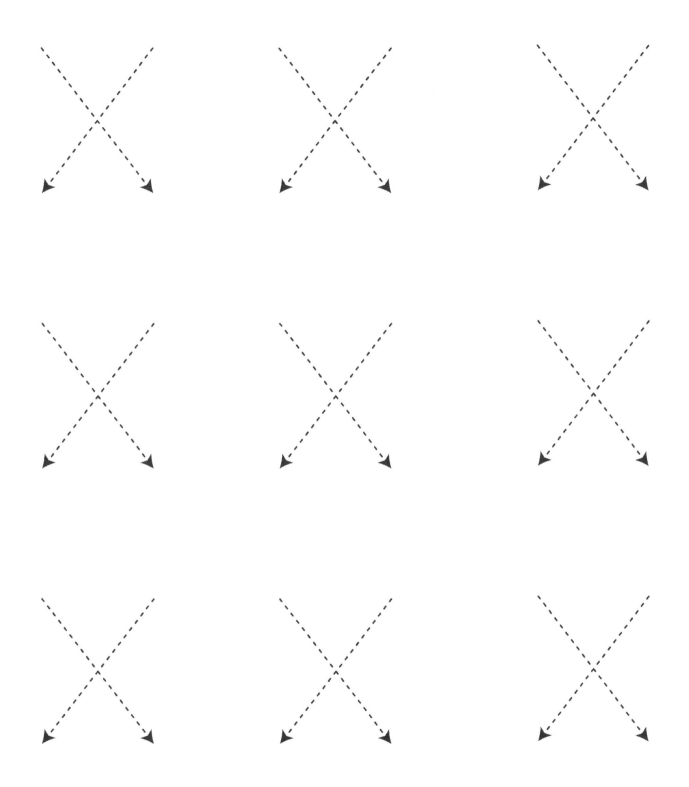

Trace the lines and patterns

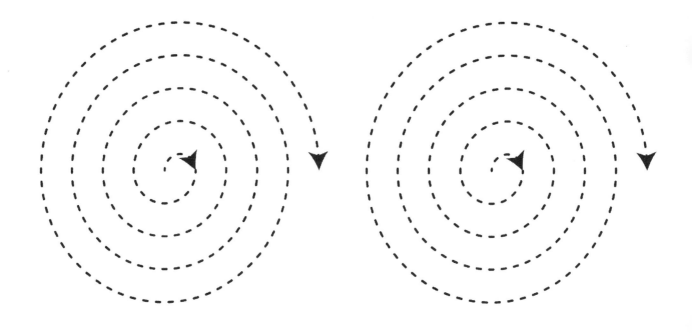

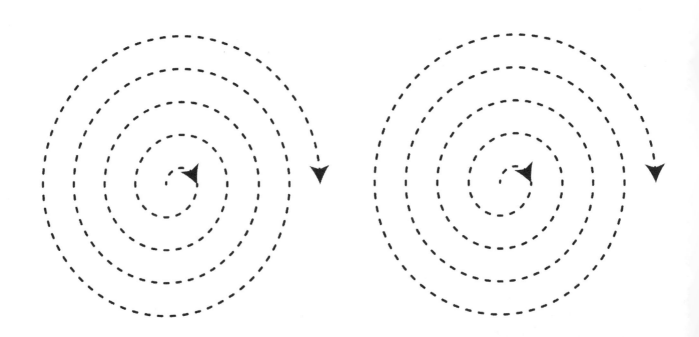

Trace the lines and patterns

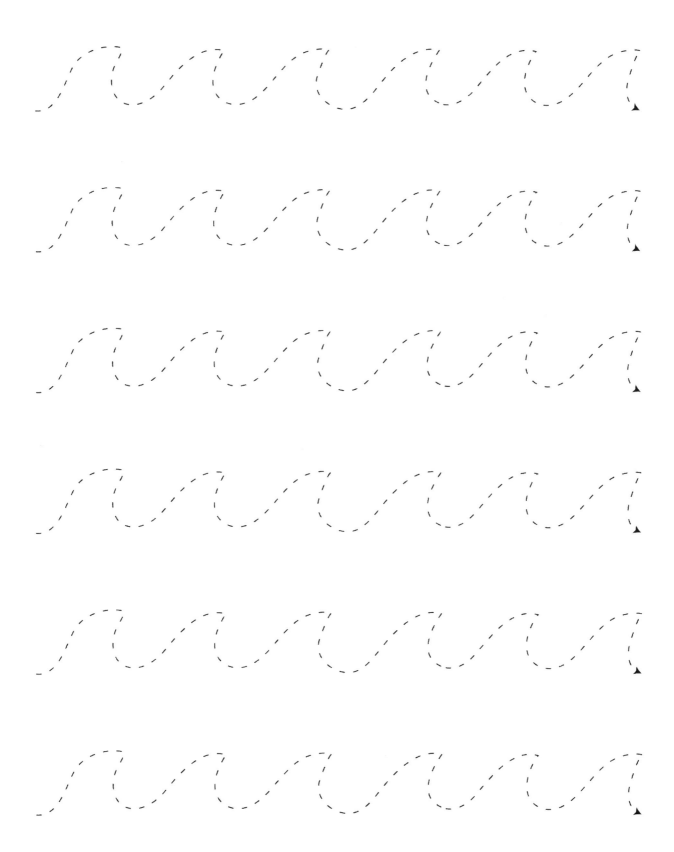

Chapter 2

Letters

Welcome to Chapter 2 of our writing journey! In this chapter, we'll be your trusty guides as we embark on the adventure of learning how to write the perfect letters. We'll break down each step, making it easy and enjoyable for you to create beautifully formed characters. By the end of this chapter, you'll have the skills to write letters with style and precision. So, let's grab our pencils or pens and dive into the world of perfect penmanship – you're about to become a master of the written word!

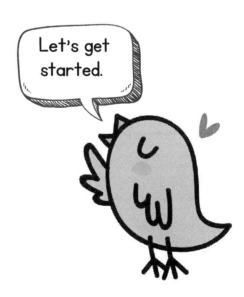

Print Alphabet

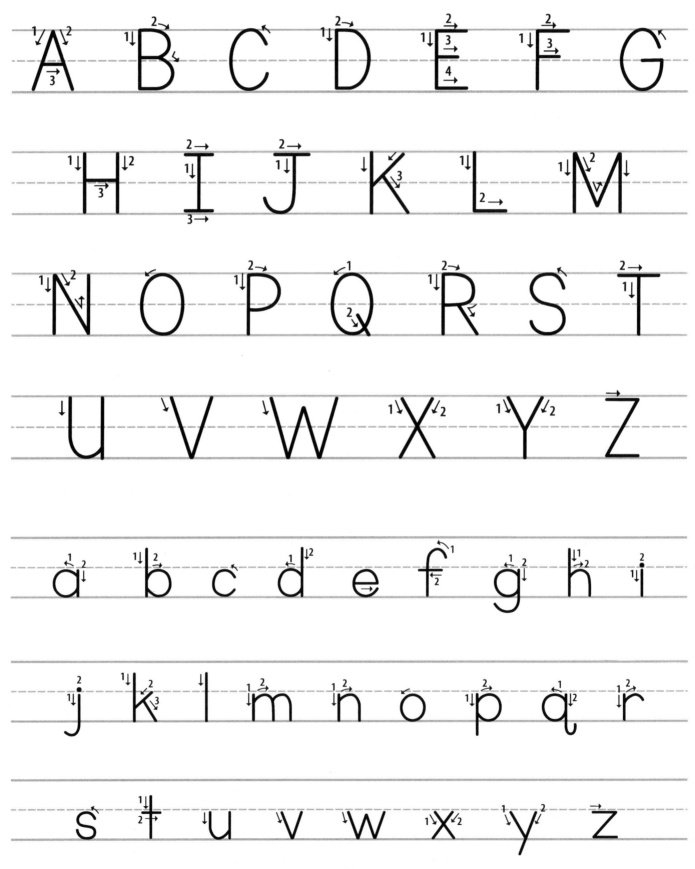

Aa

Follow the dots to trace the letters, then write them neatly in the open space provided.

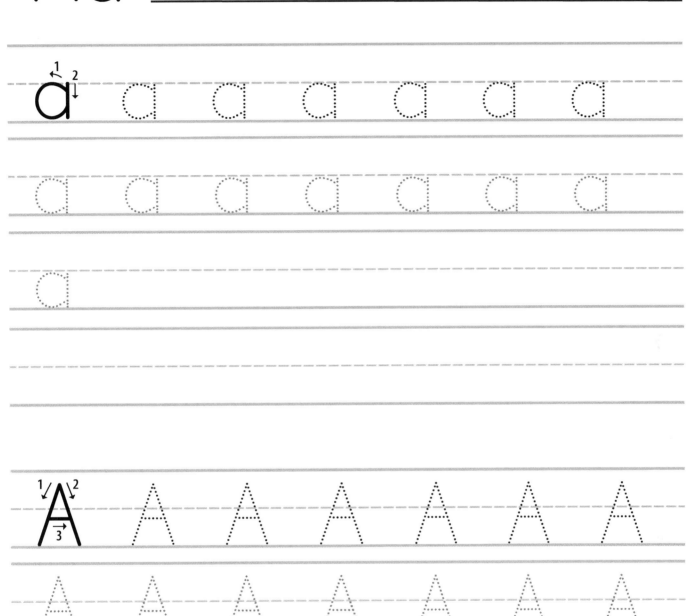

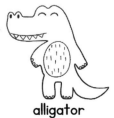

A B C D E F G H I J K L M N O P Q R S T U V W X Y Z

alligator

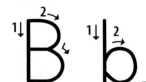

Follow the dots to trace the letters, then write them neatly in the open space provided.

bear

A B C D E F G H I J K L M N O P Q R S T U V W X Y Z

Cc

Follow the dots to trace the letters, then write them neatly in the open space provided.

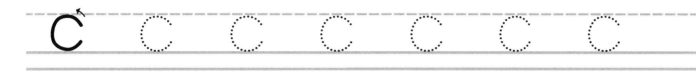
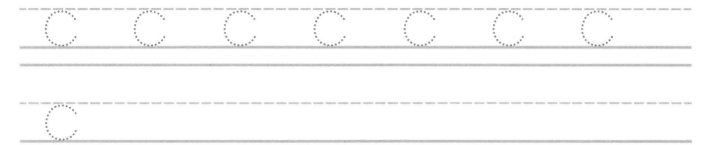
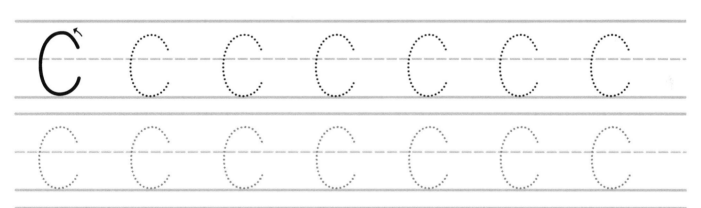
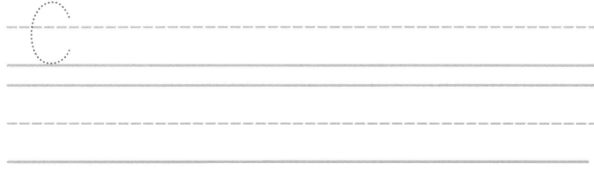

cat

A B **C** D E F G H I J K L M N O P Q R S T U V W X Y Z

Dd

Follow the dots to trace the letters, then write them neatly in the open space provided.

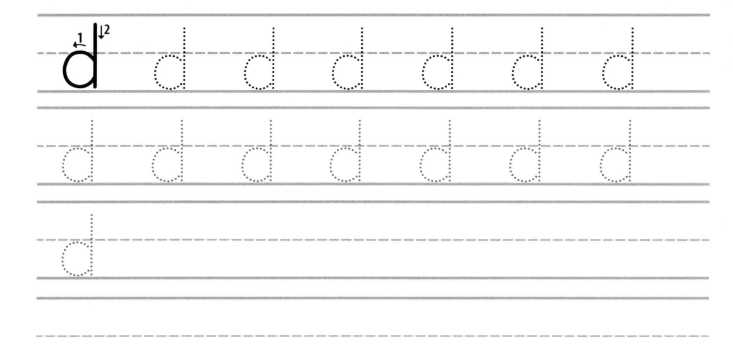

deer

A B C D E F G H I J K L M N O P Q R S T U V W X Y Z

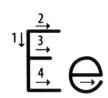

Follow the dots to trace the letters, then write them neatly in the open space provided.

A B C D E F G H I J K L M N O P Q R S T U V W X Y Z

elephant

Follow the dots to trace the letters, then write them neatly in the open space provided.

A B C D E **F** G H I J K L M N O P Q R S T U V W X Y Z

flamingo

Gg

Follow the dots to trace the letters, then write them neatly in the open space provided.

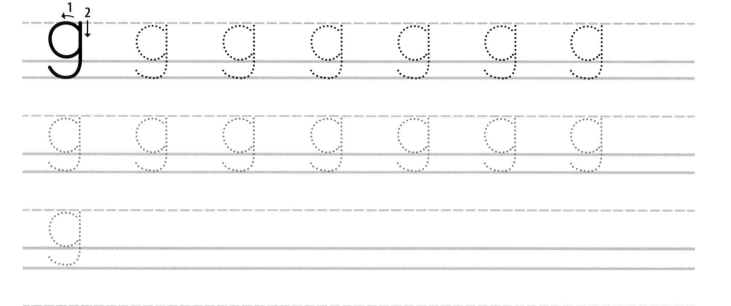

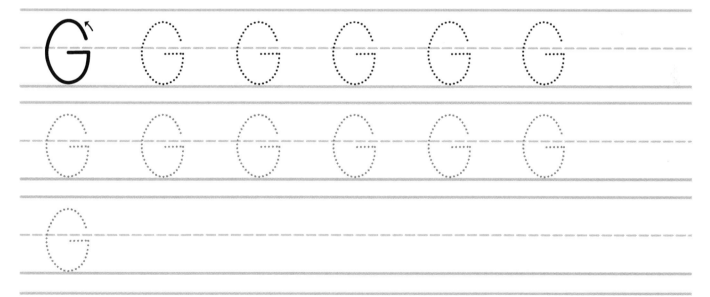

A B C D E F **G** H I J K L M N O P Q R S T U V W X Y Z

goat

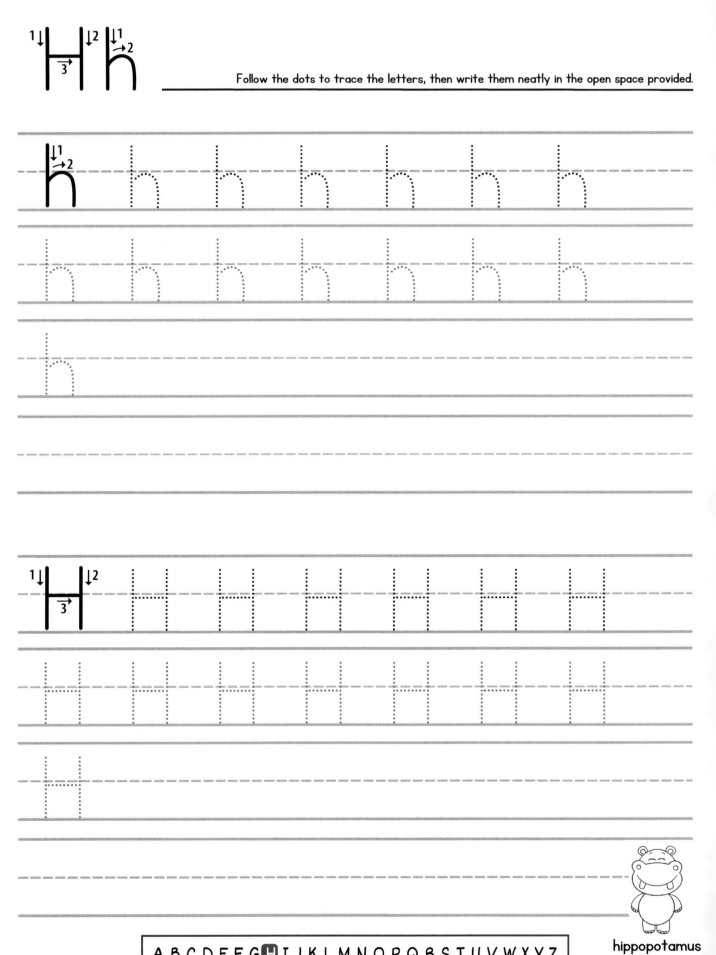

Follow the dots to trace the letters, then write them neatly in the open space provided.

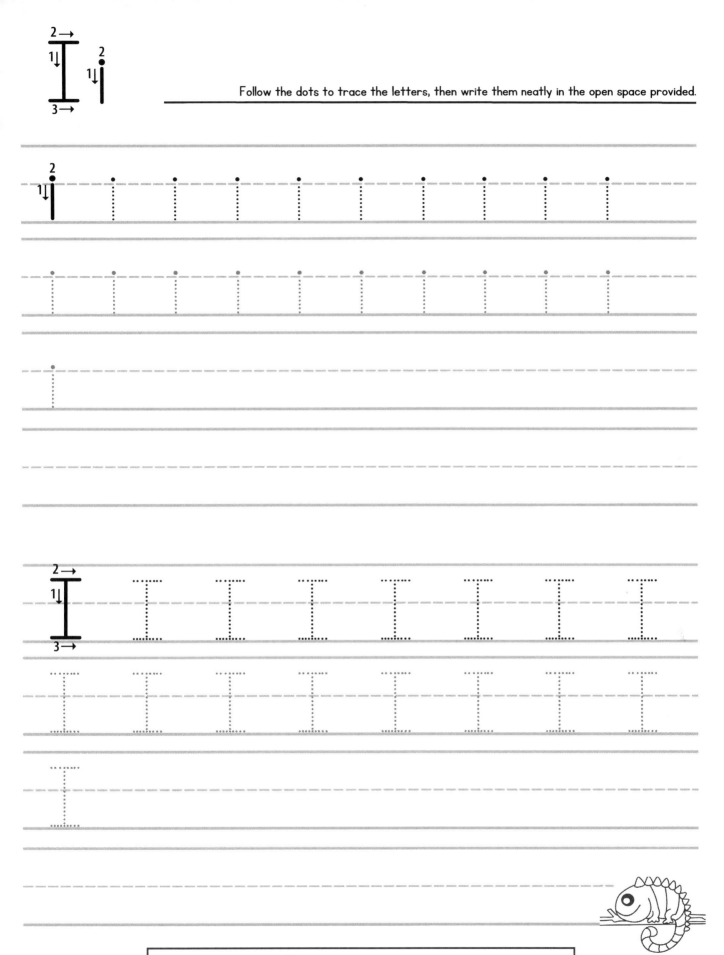

iguana

A B C D E F G H I J K L M N O P Q R S T U V W X Y Z

Follow the dots to trace the letters, then write them neatly in the open space provided.

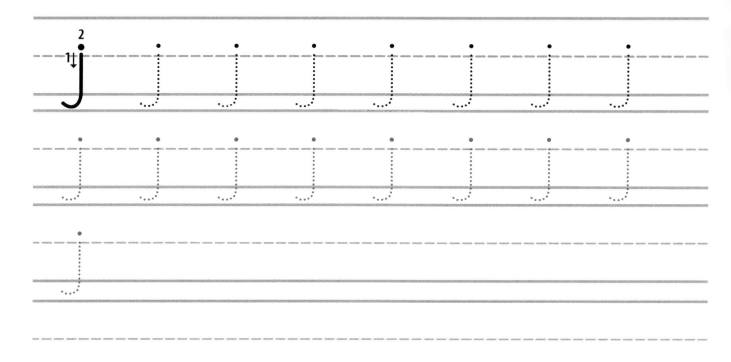
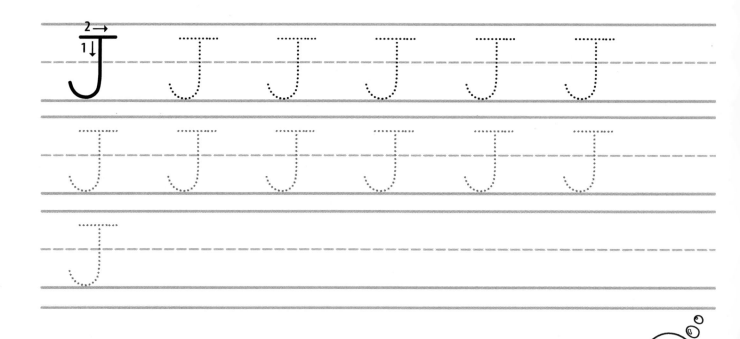

jellyfish

A B C D E F G H I J K L M N O P Q R S T U V W X Y Z

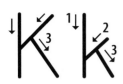

Follow the dots to trace the letters, then write them neatly in the open space provided.

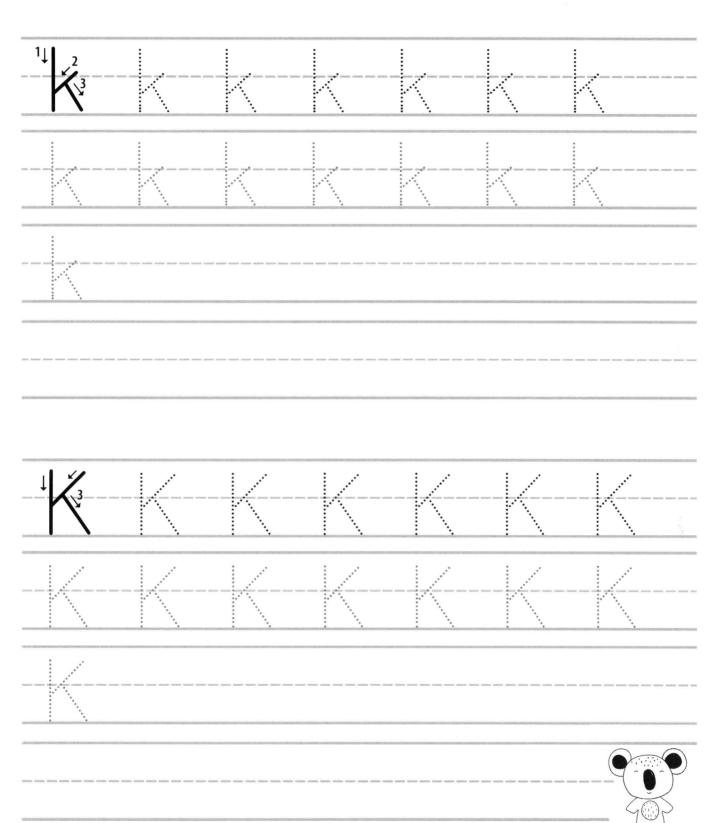

koala

A B C D E F G H I J K L M N O P Q R S T U V W X Y Z

Follow the dots to trace the letters, then write them neatly in the open space provided.

ABCDEFGHIJK**L**MNOPQRSTUVWXYZ

lion

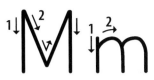

Follow the dots to trace the letters, then write them neatly in the open space provided.

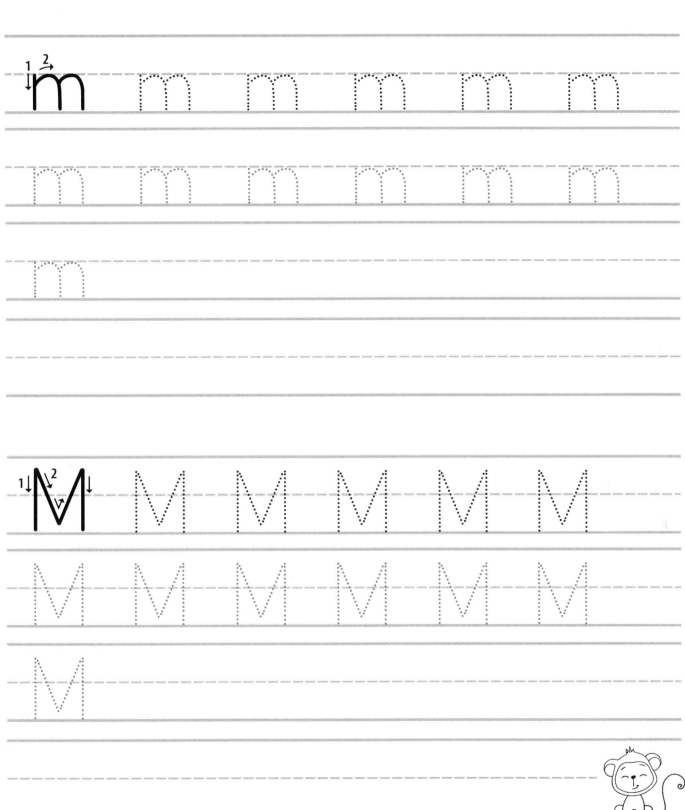

monkey

A B C D E F G H I J K L M N O P Q R S T U V W X Y Z

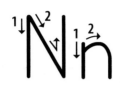

Follow the dots to trace the letters, then write them neatly in the open space provided.

A B C D E F G H I J K L M N O P Q R S T U V W X Y Z

narwhal

Oo

Follow the dots to trace the letters, then write them neatly in the open space provided.

A B C D E F G H I J K L M N **O** P Q R S T U V W X Y Z

octopus

P p

Follow the dots to trace the letters, then write them neatly in the open space provided.

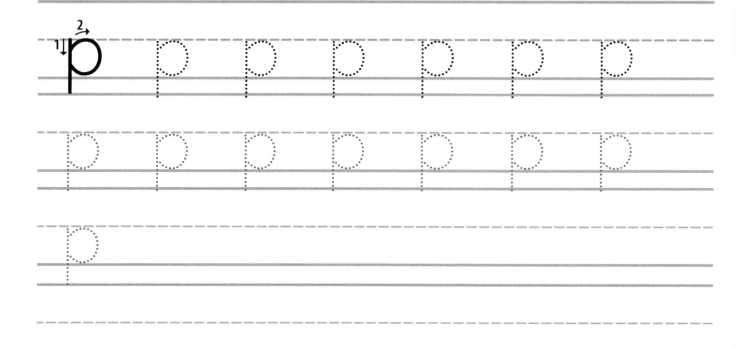

pig

A B C D E F G H I J K L M N O P Q R S T U V W X Y Z

Follow the dots to trace the letters, then write them neatly in the open space provided.

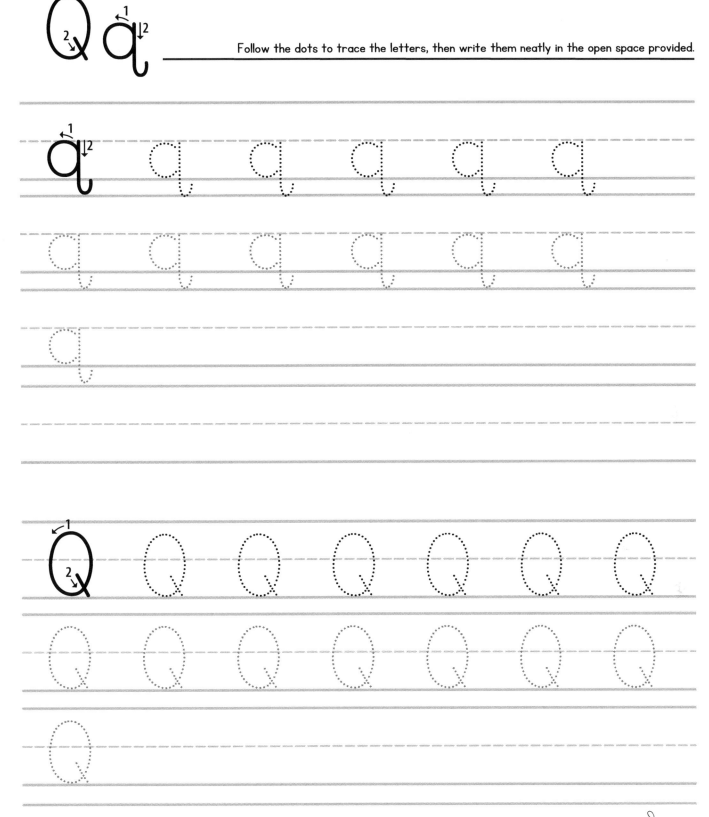

quail

A B C D E F G H I J K L M N O P Q R S T U V W X Y Z

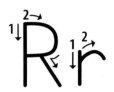

Follow the dots to trace the letters, then write them neatly in the open space provided.

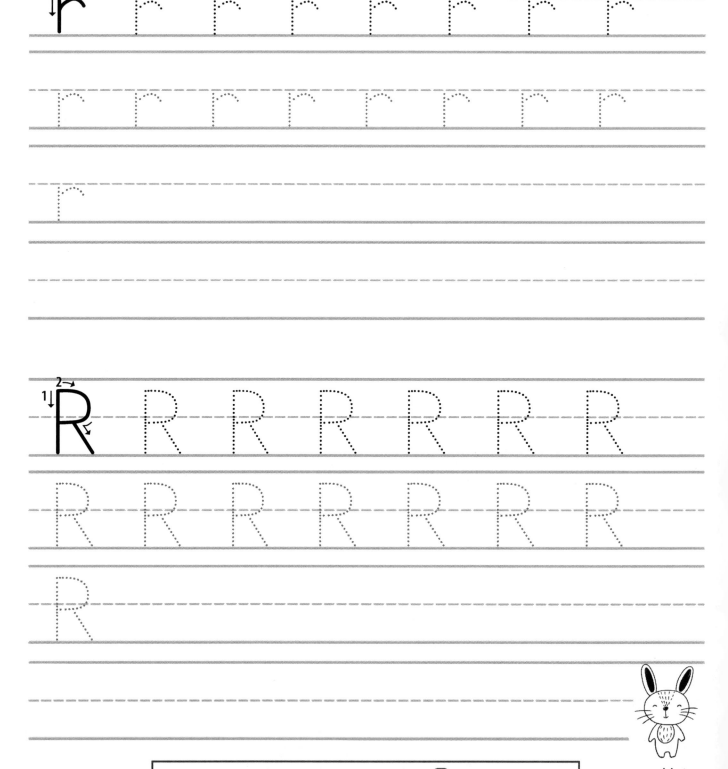

A B C D E F G H I J K L M N O P Q R S T U V W X Y Z

rabbit

Ss

Follow the dots to trace the letters, then write them neatly in the open space provided.

snake

A B C D E F G H I J K L M N O P Q R S T U V W X Y Z

Follow the dots to trace the letters, then write them neatly in the open space provided.

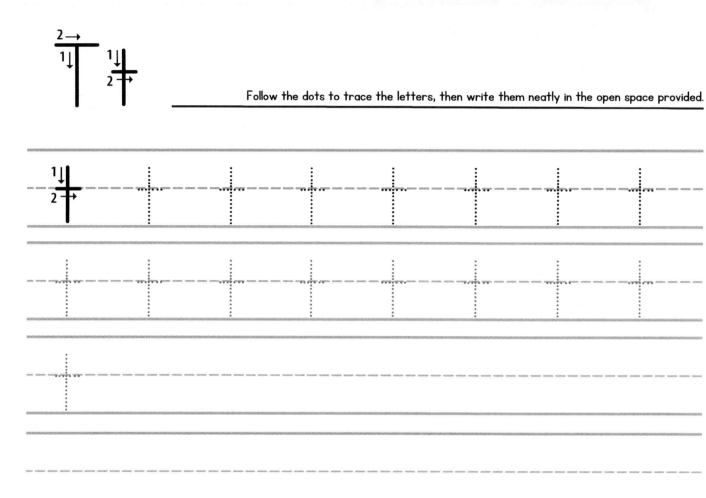

A B C D E F G H I J K L M N O P Q R S T U V W X Y Z

turtle

U u

Follow the dots to trace the letters, then write them neatly in the open space provided.

unicorn

A B C D E F G H I J K L M N O P Q R S T U V W X Y Z

Vv

Follow the dots to trace the letters, then write them neatly in the open space provided.

ABCDEFGHIJKLMNOPQRSTU**V**WXYZ

vulture

W w

Follow the dots to trace the letters, then write them neatly in the open space provided.

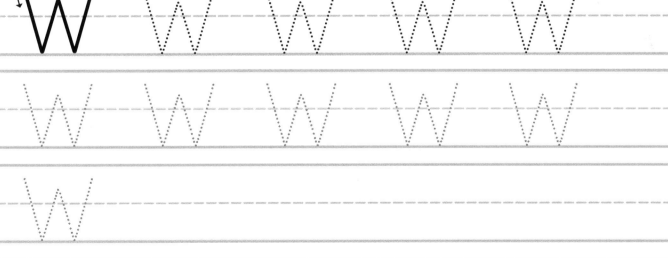

A B C D E F G H I J K L M N O P Q R S T U V **W** X Y Z

whale

Follow the dots to trace the letters, then write them neatly in the open space provided.

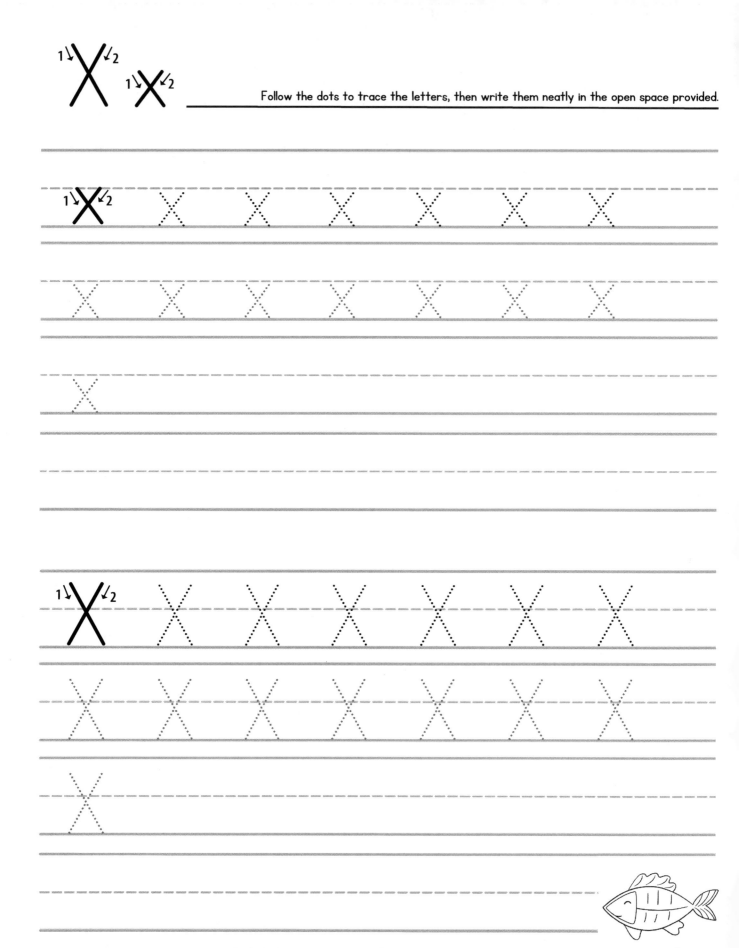

x-ray fish

A B C D E F G H I J K L M N O P Q R S T U V W X Y Z

Yy Follow the dots to trace the letters, then write them neatly in the open space provided.

A B C D E F G H I J K L M N O P Q R S T U V W X Y Z

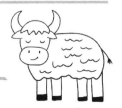
yak

Zz

Follow the dots to trace the letters, then write them neatly in the open space provided.

Z Z Z Z Z Z Z

Z Z Z Z Z Z

Z

Z Z Z Z Z Z Z

Z Z Z Z Z Z Z

Z

A B C D E F G H I J K L M N O P Q R S T U V W X Y Z

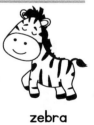

zebra

Chapter 3

Drawing and Writing

In Chapter Three, we're going to have a great time creating words and sentences! But before we begin, let's have some fun drawing interesting animals. After that, we'll trace and write three fascinating facts about each animal. Are you ready for this exciting adventure in writing and drawing?

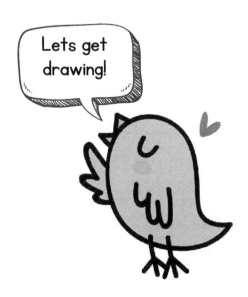

How to draw a bee.

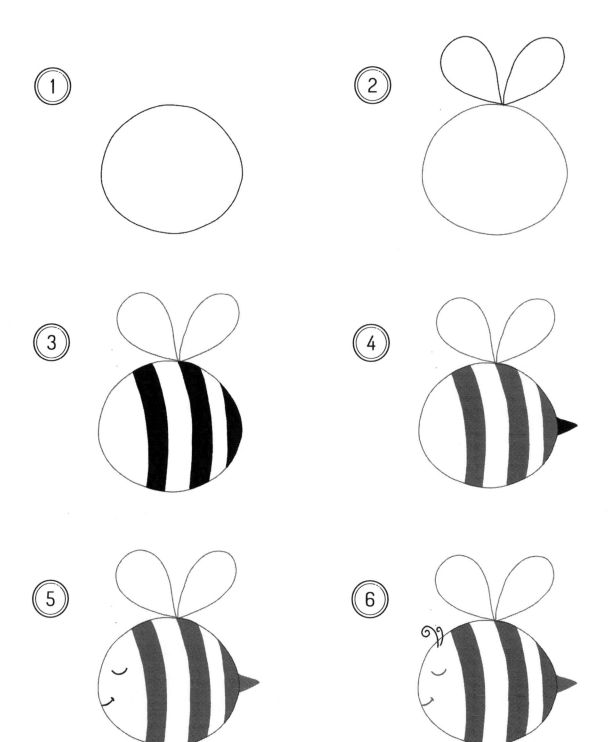

Your Turn: Draw a bee.

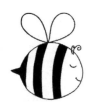

Trace the three fun facts about bees.

Bees communicate by dancing. Bees have a special dance to tell their hive mates where to find food.

Bees have fuzzy bodies. Their tiny hairs help them collect and carry pollen from one flower to another.

A single honeybee can visit up to 1,500 flowers in just one day.

Your turn: Write the three fun facts about bees.

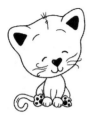# How to draw a cat.

 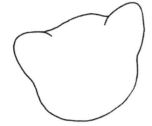

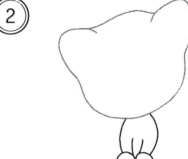

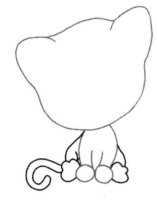

 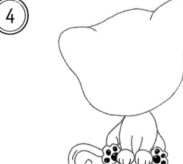

 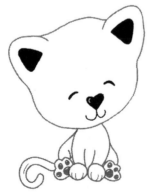

 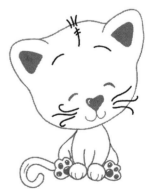

Your Turn: Draw a cat.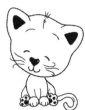

Trace the three fun facts about cats.

Cats love their sleep. On average, cats sleep for about 12 to 16 hours a day, making them true nap champions.

Cats are masters of flexibility. They have a collarbone that allows them to fit through tiny spaces.

Cats have incredible senses. Their whiskers are like magic wands, helping them sense their surroundings.

Your turn: Write the three fun facts about cats.

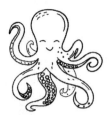

How to draw an octopus.

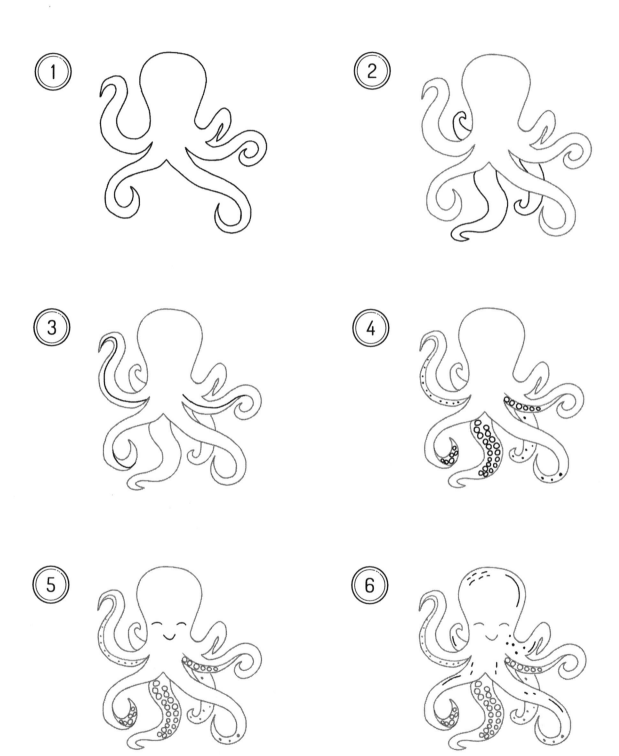

_____ Your Turn: Draw an octopus.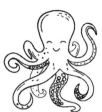

Trace the three fun facts about octopuses.

Octopuses can change color and texture to hide from predators or sneak up on prey.

Their intelligence is distributed across a brain in their head and smaller "brains" in each of their arms.

Octopuses have three hearts, two for their gills and one for the rest of their body.

Your turn: Write the three fun facts about octopuses.

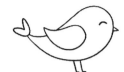 How to draw a bird.

 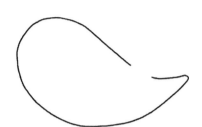

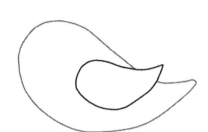

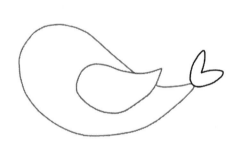

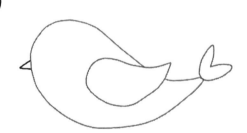

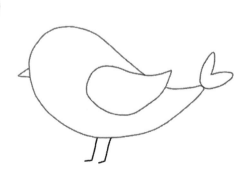

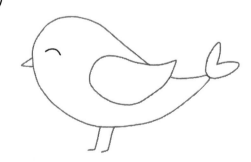

Your Turn: Draw a bird.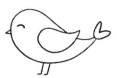

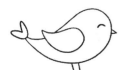

Trace the three fun facts about birds.

Some birds travel thousands of miles, using the sun, stars, and even Earth's magnetic field to find their way.

Birds are great singers. They use their voices to communicate with each other and to attract mates.

Not all birds can fly. Some, like penguins and ostriches, are excellent swimmers or runners instead.

Your turn: Write the three fun facts about birds.

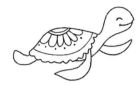 How to draw a turtle.

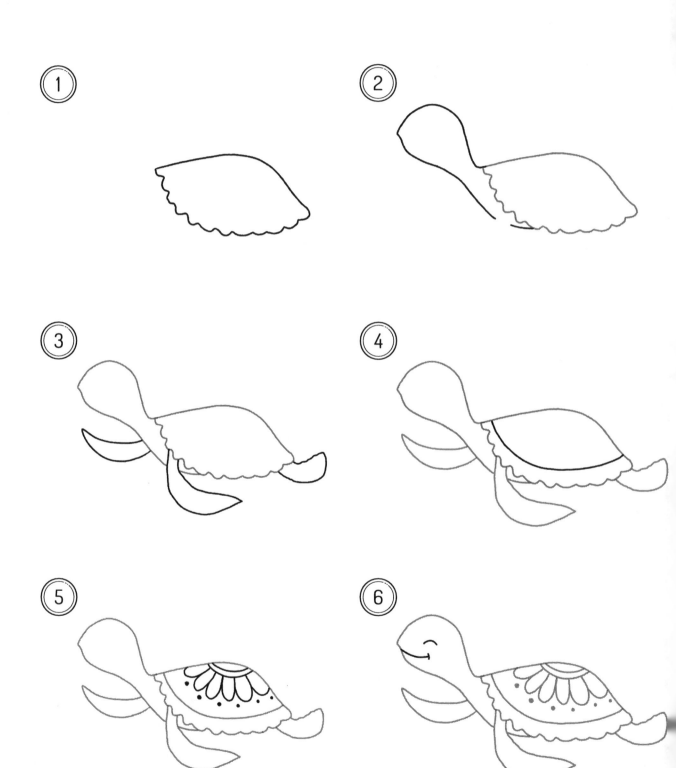

_____ Your Turn: Draw a turtle.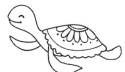

Trace the three fun facts about turtles.

Turtles are among the oldest reptiles, with a history spanning over 200 million years.

Turtles come in two main shell varieties - hard and bony, or soft. Soft - shelled turtles are agile swimmers.

Many turtles are known for their remarkable longevity, with some individuals living over 100 years.

Your turn: Write the three fun facts about turtles.

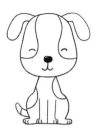

How to draw a dog.

 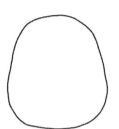 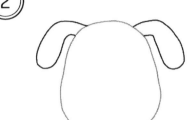

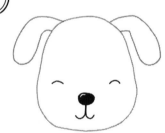 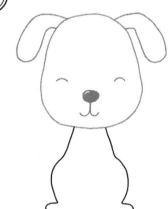

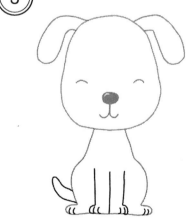 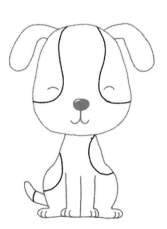

Your Turn: Draw a dog.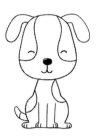

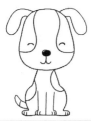

Trace the three fun facts about dogs.

Dogs have an incredible sense of smell, and some breeds are used in search and rescue operations.

Just like human fingerprints, each dog has a distinct nose print.

Dogs communicate through barking, howling, and other vocalizations to express their emotions and needs.

Your turn: Write the three fun facts about dogs.

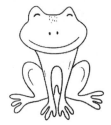

How to draw a frog.

 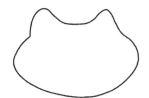

 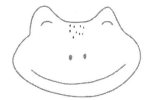 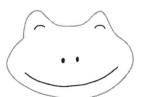

 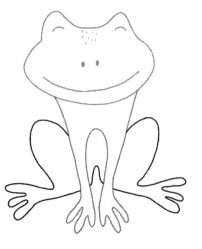 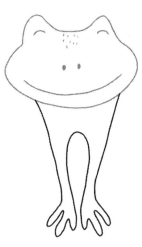

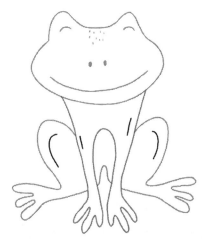

64

Your Turn: Draw a frog.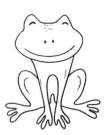

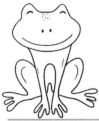

Trace the three fun facts about frogs.

Frogs can leap up to 20 times their body length.

Frogs breathe through their skin, which helps when they hibernate underwater.

Frogs have unique, fast-acting tongues to catch prey.

Your turn: Write the three fun facts about frogs.

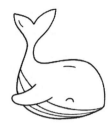 How to draw a whale.

 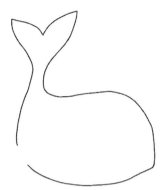

 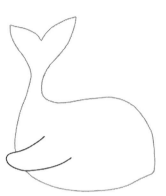

 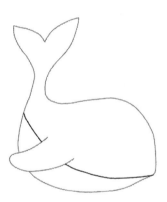

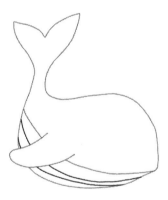

 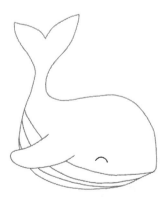

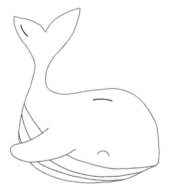

Your Turn: Draw a whale.

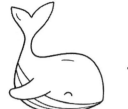

Trace the three fun facts about whales.

Blue whales have hearts as heavy as cars and arteries large enough for a person to stand in.

Humpback whales travel thousands of miles between their feeding and breeding areas.

Whales use complex songs and dialects to communicate within their pods.

Your turn: Write the three fun facts about whales.

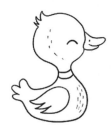 How to draw a duck.

 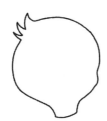

 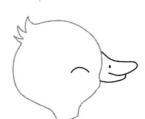

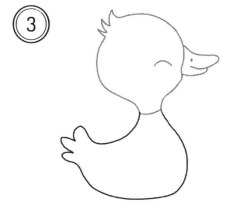

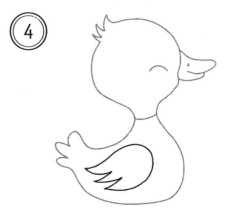

 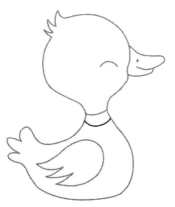

 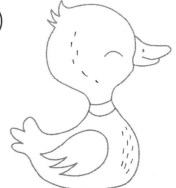

_____ Your Turn: Draw a duck.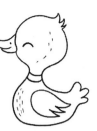

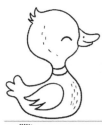

Trace the three fun facts about ducks.

Ducks have waterproof feathers that keep them dry while swimming.

Ducks come in over 120 unique species, from small teals to large mallards.

Ducks are skilled at either dabbling near the water's surface or diving deep to find their food.

Your turn: Write the three fun facts about ducks.

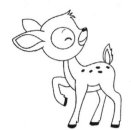

How to draw a deer.

①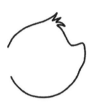

②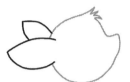

③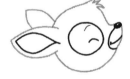

④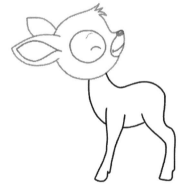

⑤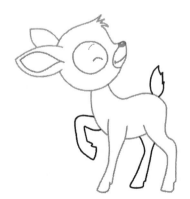

⑥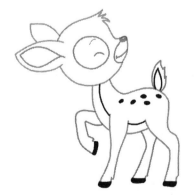

Your Turn: Draw a deer.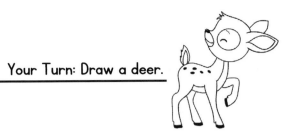

Trace the three fun facts about deer.

Male deer grow and shed their antlers annually, which can be quite impressive.

Deer are surprisingly good swimmers and can cover long distances in the water.

Deer have a four-compartment stomach that allows them to efficiently digest their plant-based diet.

Your turn: Write the three fun facts about deer.

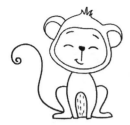 How to draw a monkey.

①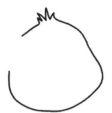

②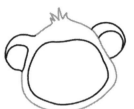

③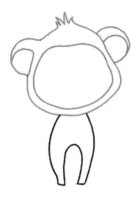

④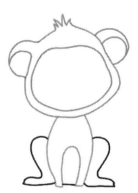

⑤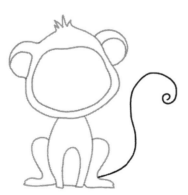

⑥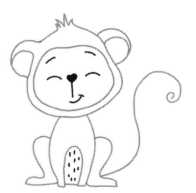

Your Turn: draw a monkey.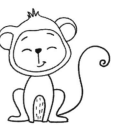

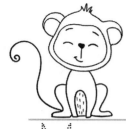

Trace the three fun facts about monkeys.

Monkeys have tails of different lengths and types to suit their lifestyles.

Monkeys are highly social, living in groups with complex hierarchies for protection and foraging.

Some monkey species, like capuchins and macaques, use tools to find food.

Your turn: Write the three fun facts about monkeys.

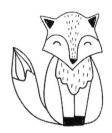 How to draw a fox.

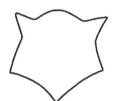

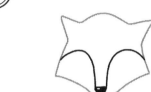

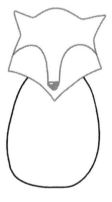

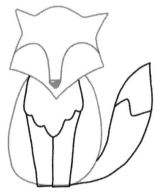

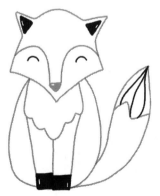

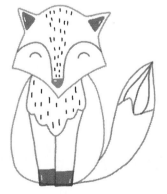

Your Turn: Draw a fox.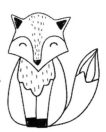

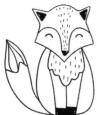

Trace the three fun facts about foxes.

Foxes are clever. They are known for their intelligence and ability to outsmart other animals.

Foxes can be found all over the world. There are about 37 different species of foxes.

Foxes are fast runners. They can run up to 30 miles per hour.

Your turn: Write the three fun facts about foxes.

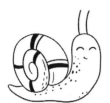 How to draw a snail.

 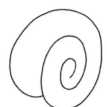

 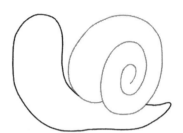

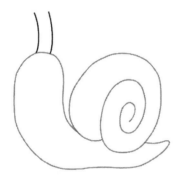 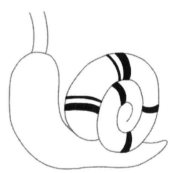

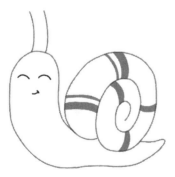 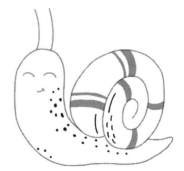

Your Turn: draw a snail.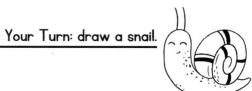

Trace the three fun facts about snails.

Snails are famously slow, moving just a few inches per minute with the help of a slime trail.

Snails carry their protective shells made of calcium carbonate, which they can retreat into when needed.

Snails often come out at night to avoid predators and maintain moisture.

Your turn: Write the three fun facts about snails.

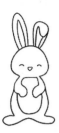 How to draw a rabbit.

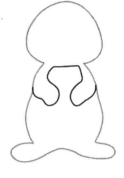

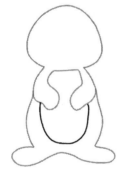

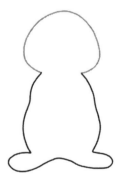

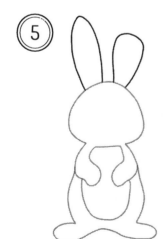

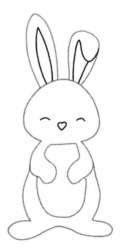

Your Turn: Draw a rabbit.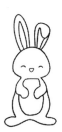

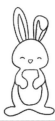

Trace the three fun facts about rabbits.

Rabbits breed rapidly, with the potential for a single pair to produce 184,000 descendants in 7 years.

Rabbits can jump high and far, reaching up to 36 inches high and 10 feet far.

Many rabbits are most active during dawn and dusk, helping them evade predators.

Your turn: Write the three fun facts about rabbits.

Chapter 4

Free Writing

Chapter Four is all about getting creative! Each page is set up with blank spaces for drawing and lined areas for writing. These pages are your opportunity to let your imagination run wild, whether you're crafting stories, poems, or jotting down your thoughts. So, grab your pen, let your ideas soar, and watch your words and drawings come to life on these pages. Your journey into the world of limitless creativity and improved penmanship starts right here!

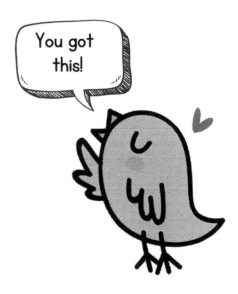